MECHANICAL COMPREHENSION
TESTS

THE **TESTING** SERIES
expert advice on test preparation

how2become

Orders: Please contact How2become Ltd,
Suite 2, 50 Churchill Square Business Centre, Kings Hill, Kent ME19 4YU.

Telephone: (44) 0845 643 1299 - Lines are open Monday to Friday 9am until 5pm. Fax: (44) 01732 525965. You can also order via the e mail address info@how2become.co.uk.

ISBN 9781909229969

First published 2012

Typeset for How2become Ltd by Molly Hill, Canada.

Printed in Great Britain for How2become Ltd by CMP (uk) Limited, Dorset.

WELCOME

Dear Sir/Madam,

Welcome to *Mechanical Comprehension Tests*. This guide has been designed to help you prepare for any mechanical aptitude test. We feel certain that you will find the guide both a comprehensive and highly informative tool for helping you pass this type of test.

Mechanical Comprehension Tests are an assessment tool used for measuring a candidate's ability to perceive and understand the relationship of physical forces and mechanical elements in practical situations. This aptitude is important in jobs and training programs that require the understanding and application of mechanical principles. The types of jobs which will normally require this level of ability include practical jobs such as train driver, firefighter, some armed forces roles, engineering roles and other similar jobs where an ability to work with mechanical concepts is crucial.

In addition to the tests within this guide we would also like to give you **FREE ACCESS** to our online psychometric testing facility.

To gain access to our suite, simply go to the following website:

www.PsychometricTestsOnline.co.uk

If you would like any further assistance with any career selection process then we offer the following products and training courses via the website www.how2become.com:

• How to join the Army, RAF, Royal Navy, Royal Marines and Parachute Regiment.

THE **TESTING** SERIES

- How to become a Train Driver, Firefighter or Police Officer.
- How to pass psychometric tests, numerical reasoning and verbal comprehension tests.
- Career training courses.

Finally, you won't achieve much in life without hard work, determination and perseverance. Work hard, stay focused and be what you want!

Good luck and best wishes,

The how2become team

The How2become team

PREFACE
BY RICHARD MCMUNN

Before we get into the guide and I provide you with a number of sample mechanical comprehension tests, it is important that I explain a little bit about my background and why I am qualified to help you succeed.

I joined the Royal Navy soon after leaving school and spent four fabulous years in the Fleet Air Arm branch on-board HMS Invincible. It had always been my dream to become a Firefighter and I only ever intended staying in the Royal Navy for the minimum amount of time. During the selection process for joining the Royal Navy I was required to undertake a mechanical comprehension test. I can remember at the time I found it to be quite a tough test, simply because I had very little work experience and there were also very few practice papers around for me to try. However, I applied a level of common-sense and I passed the test with good grades. As I progressed through my career in the Royal Navy as an aircraft engineer I realised how important an understanding of mechanical concepts was to my job. You will find the tests within the guide useful in helping you prepare for careers which require a level of mechanical aptitude.

At the age of 21 I left the Royal Navy and joined Kent Fire and Rescue Service. Over the next 17 years I had an amazing career with a fantastic organisation. During that time I was heavily involved in training and recruitment, often sitting on interview panels and marking application forms for those people who wanted to become Firefighters. I also worked very hard and rose to the rank of Station Manager. I passed numerous assessment centres during my time in the job and I estimate that I was successful at over 95% of interviews I attended. It was ironic that I also had to pass a mechanical comprehension test when I joined the Fire Service; however, by the time applied for this job I was very competent in mechanical aptitude, as you can imagine.

The reason for my success in both the Royal Navy and the Fire Service was not because I am special in anyway, or that I have lots of educational qualifications, because I don't. In the build-up to every job application or promotion I always prepared myself thoroughly.

Over the past few years I have taught many people how to prepare for career selection processes and assessment centres. The way to pass mechanical comprehension tests is to embark on a comprehensive period of intense preparation. I would also urge you to use an action plan during your preparation. This will allow you to focus your mind on exactly what you need to do in order to pass your test or assessment. For example, if it has been many years since you last attended a test, then you will probably have to do a lot of work to do in this area. You can do this by trying out, and understanding, the test questions and answers within this workbook and also by gaining access to our free online psychometric testing facility at the following website:

www.PsychometricTestsOnline.co.uk

The above testing suite is free of charge so I would urge you to use it during your preparation.

Finally, it is very important that you believe in your own abilities. It does not matter if you have no qualifications. It does not matter if you have no knowledge yet of how to pass mechanical comprehension tests. What does matter is self-belief, self-discipline and a genuine desire to improve and become successful.

Enjoy trying out the tests in the guide and I wish you all the success in the future!

Best wishes,

Richard McMunn

Richard McMunn

Disclaimer

Every effort has been made to ensure that the information contained within this guide is accurate at the time of publication. How2become Ltd is not responsible for anyone failing any part of any selection process as a result of the information contained within this guide. How2become Ltd and their authors cannot accept any responsibility for any errors or omissions within this guide, however caused. No responsibility for loss or damage occasioned by any person acting, or refraining from action, as a result f the material in this publication can be accepted by How2become Ltd.

The information within this guide does not represent the views of any third party service or organisation.

ABOUT MECHANICAL COMPREHENSION TESTS

Mechanical comprehension or aptitude tests have been in use for many years as a method for assessing a candidates potential to perform a specific job. Predominantly, they are used in careers which require an ability to work with, or understand, mechanical concepts. Examples of types of careers which require this level of aptitude include:

- Train driver

- Driving careers

- Armed forces jobs

- Engineering careers

- Emergency services

- Motor mechanic

- Aircraft engineer

Of course, the above list is not exhaustive and there are many other jobs which require an ability to interpret mechanical concepts.

Some mechanical comprehension tests include fault diagnosis questions which are used to select personnel for technical roles where they need to be able to find and repair faults in different operating systems. I have deliberately not included these types of questions within this guide as they are being used less and less. However, for those people who wish to try these tests, and indeed different types of psychometric tests, please access he free facility at www.PsychometricTestsOnline.co.uk.

Many mechanical comprehension tests require you to concentrate on 'principles' rather than on making calculations, and as such will include diagrams and pictures as part of the question. For example, you may be shown a diagram of a series of cogs and be asked to work out which way a specific cog is turning if another one rotates either clockwise or anticlockwise. Please do not be offended by me confirming with you that you understand the terms clockwise and anticlockwise. Understanding these two very simple terms is crucial to answering mechanical comprehension test questions accurately. For those people who are unsure, here's an explanation:

CLOCKWISE AND ANTICLOCKWISE

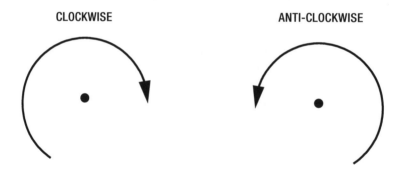

The easiest way to remember the above is to think of the way that the hands on a clock rotate; hence the phrase 'clockwise'.

You may also find that some test questions which have been created in the USA refer to anticlockwise as counterclockwise.

UNDERSTANDING MECHANICAL ADVANTAGE

You may find that some mechanical comprehension tests ask you to calculate the mechanical advantage of a simple pulley system.

Here's an explanation of how mechanical advantage works when using a simple pulley system.

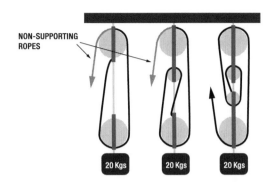

EXAMPLES OF SIMPLE PULLEY SYSTEMS

If you study the three pulley systems above you will note that each system has both supporting ropes and non-supporting ropes. Supporting ropes are ones which, as the name suggests, support the load. Only the first two pulley systems have non-supporting ropes which I have indicated.

The non-supporting ropes in the first two pulley systems above simply change the direction of the force.

To calculate the mechanical advantage in a moveable pulley system, we simply have to count the number of supporting ropes. Counting the supporting ropes in the pulley systems above, the mechanical advantage of each of system is, from left to right 2, 3, and 5.

In order to demonstrate further the concept of mechanical advantage using simple pulley systems, please try the following sample four questions to see how you get on.

Question 1
What is the mechanical advantage?

Answer [   ]

Question 2

What is the mechanical advantage?

Answer

Question 3

What is the mechanical advantage?

Answer

Question 4

What is the mechanical advantage?

Answer

ANSWERS TO SAMPLE MECHANICAL ADVANTAGE QUESTIONS

Q1. For this simple pulley system there is just one supporting rope. Therefore, the mechanical advantage is 1.

Q2. In this pulley system there are two supporting ropes and the mechanical advantage is 2.

Q3. In question 3 you will notice that the pulley is not attached directly to the beam. This is known as a moveable pulley system whereby the pulley is attached to the load/weight. When the rope is pulled up the weight/load will also move up. You will notice that the weight is supported by both the rope end attached to the upper beam and the end which will be held by the person. Each side of the rope is now supporting the weight; therefore, each side carries only half the weight. The mechanical advantage of this system is 2.

Q4. In question 4 there are four supporting ropes and one non-supporting rope. The mechanical advantage here is 4.

The pulley systems I have used in the example questions are called simple pulley systems. The reason for this title is because they utilise the same rope for the entire system. Pulley systems which are attached using more than one rope (not one continuous rope), are more complex. You will find that the vast majority of mechanical comprehension tests for regular jobs will use simple pulley systems.

Of course, pulley systems are only one type of question you will encounter when sitting mechanical comprehension tests. Within the sample tests sections of this workbook I have tried to provide you with a cross-section of questions to give you a better understanding of what the test questions may look like. Let's now take a look at some tips that will help you to perform to the best of your ability when sitting mechanical comprehension tests.

TIPS FOR PASSING MECHANICAL COMPREHENSION TESTS

> The majority of employers will assess you on speed and accuracy. Therefore, you are advised against random 'guessing'. Over the years it has become common practice for test-takes to wildly guess when taking tests that are multiple-choice in nature, especially towards the end of the test when they are running out of time. In order to stop this practice more and more test administrators are deducting marks for incorrect answers. Therefore, during your preparation for your assessment I recommend you simply practice lots of test questions but more importantly understand how the answer is reached.

> Whilst on the subject of multiple-choice questions, you will most probably find that there are more mechanical comprehension test questions than you can answer during the allocated time given for the test. If this is the case, do not worry. Many tests are design so that you do not finish them. Once again, simply work as fast as you can but also aim for accuracy.

> If you come up against a difficult question during your mechanical comprehension test, move on, but remember to leave a gap on the answer sheet. If you fail to leave a gap then each of the preceding answers will be incorrect.

> In the build-up to the test, if you feel like you are struggling with basic mechanical concepts then I recommend you study a car manual such as Haynes. This will give you an idea of how mechanical concepts work. You can obtain Haynes manuals at www.haynes.co.uk.

> I get asked on many occasions what is the pass mark for the test I am sitting? Whilst many test administrators will set a pass mark of 70% the simple answer is I do not know. This is because it is not uncommon for an employer or test administrator to set the pass mark based on an average score for the group of people taking the test. This enables the employer or test administrator to pick the upper quartile of test takers, ensuring they get the cream of the crop. The other matter to consider is that your scores in the mechanical comprehension test will normally go towards you overall score in an assessment; so, if you don't do too well in one particular test this does not necessarily mean you will fail the entire assessment!

> Consider buying a GCSE Physics booklet such as 'Letts GCSE Revision Notes' (by Paul Levy – ISBN: 1840854758). I also recommend

the Mechanical Aptitude and Spatial Relation Test (Barron's Mechanical Aptitude & Spatial Relations Test) by Joel Wiesen. Both of these books are available for under £5 through Amazon.co.uk.

It's now time for you to try out the sample tests that I have created for you. There are twenty questions in each test and you have twenty minutes to complete each one of them. Answers are provided at the end of each test.

TEST 1
MECHANICAL COMPREHENSION

YOU HAVE 20 MINUTES TO COMPLETE THIS TEST.

Question 1

A block and tackle refers to a device which is used to:

    A. Place under the wheel of a car to stop it from rolling backward

    B. Catch large fish

    C. Leverage a stationary object

    D. Hoist an object upwards by means of rope and pulleys

Answer [ ]

Question 2

Which man is carrying less weight?

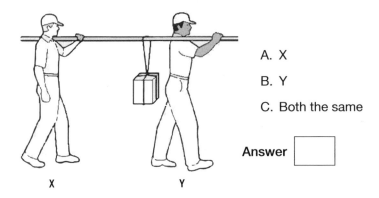

X   Y

    A. X

    B. Y

    C. Both the same

Answer [ ]

Question 3

If wheel A rotates clockwise, which of the other wheels also rotate clockwise?

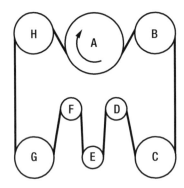

    A. All of them

    B. B, C, E, G and H

    C. D and F

    D. D, E and F

Answer [ ]

Question 4

A builder is told to pitch his ladder a third of the working height away from the building below. How many metres away from the building should the foot of the ladder be placed?

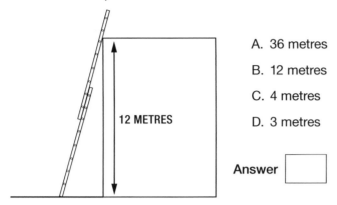

12 METRES

A. 36 metres

B. 12 metres

C. 4 metres

D. 3 metres

Answer

Question 5

What is the mechanical advantage in the diagram below?

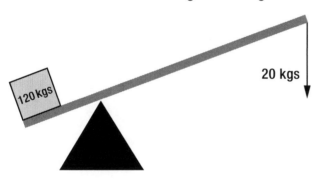

120 kgs

20 kgs

A. 2

B. 4

C. 5

D. 6

Answer

Question 6

A hot air balloon is able to float because:

    A. The hot air is turbo-charged

    B. The hot air is less dense than the external air

    C. The hot air is denser than the external air

    D. It is filled with helium

Answer

Question 7

Which of the following materials will float on water?

    A. Balsawood

    B. Glass

    C. Metal

    D. Rock

Answer

Question 8

Water is flowing into the following tank through the left-hand side inlet pipe at a rate of 18 litres per minute. If the water is flowing out through the lower right-hand side outlet pipe at a rate of 14 litres per minute, how much time will it take for the tank to overflow?

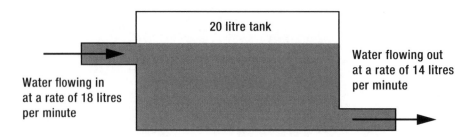

20 litre tank

Water flowing out at a rate of 14 litres per minute

Water flowing in at a rate of 18 litres per minute

A. 2 minutes

B. 3 minutes

C. 5 minutes

D. 8 minutes

Answer

Question 9

How much weight will need to be placed on the right hand side to balance the beam?

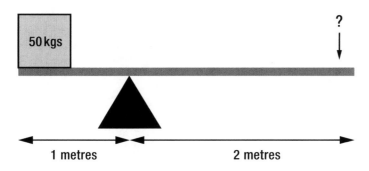

1 metres   2 metres

A. 100 Kgs

B. 200 Kgs

C. 50 Kgs

D. 25 Kgs

Answer

Question 10

If the wheel rotates anticlockwise, what will happen to X?

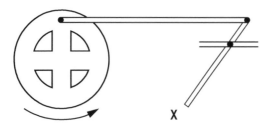

A. Move to the right and stop

B. Move to the left and stop

C. Move backwards and forwards

Answer

Question 11

Which chain will support the load on its own?

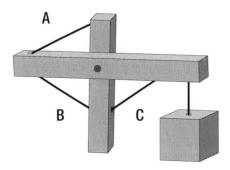

A. A

B. B

C. C

D. None of them

Answer

Question 12

Which nail is likely to pull out first?

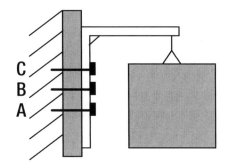

A. A

B. B

C. C

D. All of them at the same time

Answer ☐

Question 13

If wheel A rotates anticlockwise, which way and how will B rotate?

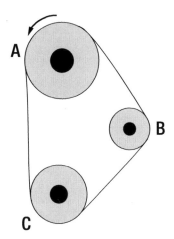

A. Clockwise faster

B. Clockwise slower

C. Anticlockwise faster

D. Anticlockwise slower

Answer ☐

Question 14

Which way and how will cog C rotate?

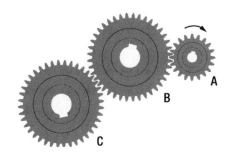

A. Clockwise faster than A

B. Clockwise slower than A

C. Anticlockwise faster than A

D. Anticlockwise slower A

Answer ☐

Question 15

Which lever will require more effort to lift the load?

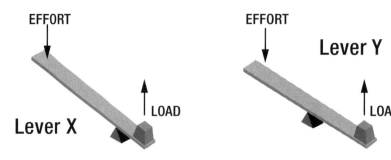

A. Lever X

B. Lever Y

C. Both the same

Answer [ ]

Question 16

How much force is required to lift the load?

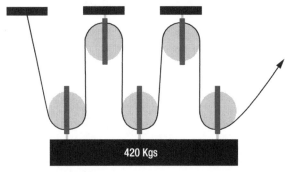

A. 140 Kgs

B. 210 Kgs

C. 90 Kgs

D. 70 Kgs

Answer [ ]

Question 17

How much weight is required to hold the load?

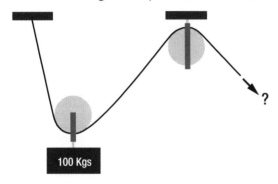

100 Kgs

   A. 400 Kgs

   B. 200 Kgs

   C. 100 Kgs

   D. 50 Kgs

Answer

Question 18

If lever A moves in the direction shown, which way will B move?

B

   A. To the left

   B. To the right

   C. Backwards and forwards

   D. It will not move

Answer

C

A

Question 19

If the motor wheel rotates in a clockwise direction, then:

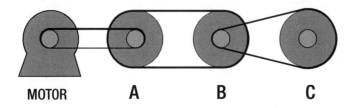

MOTOR   A   B   C

A. B and C move clockwise

B. B and C move anticlockwise

C. B moves clockwise and C moves anticlockwise

D. B moves anticlockwise, and C moves clockwise

Answer ☐

Question 20

If weight is placed on the top of each stack of boxes, which stack would support the most weight?

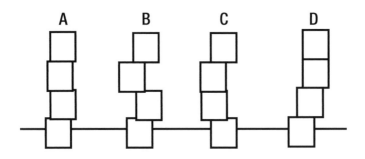

A. A

B. B

C. C

D. D

Answer ☐

THE **TESTING** SERIES

ANSWERS TO MECHANICAL COMPREHENSION TEST 1

1. D

A block and tackle is used to hoist an object upwards by means of rope and pulleys

2. X

You will see that the object is closer to man Y than man X. Therefore, man X is carrying less weight.

3. C

Wheel F and D are the only other wheels which will rotate clockwise.

4. C

The working height is 12 metres; therefore, the foot of the ladder must be placed 4 metres away from the building.

5. D

120kgs/20kgs = mechanical advantage of 6

6. B

The hot air inside a hot air balloon is less dense than the external air.

7. A

Balsawood is the only material here that will float on water.

8. C

Water is flowing in at a rate of 18 litres per minute; however, because water is also leaving the tank at a rate of 14 litres per minute, this means that only 4 litres per minute is effectively filling the tank. If the tank has a capacity of 20 litres then it will take 5 minutes for it to overflow.

9. D

In order to calculate the weight required in this type of situation you can make use of the following formula:

$f = (w \times d1)/d2$
f = force required
w = weight
$d1$ = distance 1
$d2$ = distance 2

Answer:
$f = (50 \times 1)/2$

(50/2 is the same as 25/1; the force required is 25 Kg)

10. C

It will move backwards and forwards as the wheel rotates.

11. B

Chain B is the only one which can support the load independently.

12. C

Nail C is most likely to pull out first.

13. C

Wheel B will rotate anticlockwise and faster because it is smaller than the other two wheels.

14. B

Cog C will rotate clockwise and slower than A because it has more teeth.

15. B

Lever Y will require more effort to lift the load because the fulcrum is further away from the load than level X.

16. D

The load weighs 420 Kgs and there are a total of six sections of rope supporting it. In order to calculate the force required to lift the load simply divide the weight by the number of ropes in order to reach your answer:

420 / 6 = 70 Kgs

17. D

In this scenario the weight is suspended by two pulleys. This means the weight is split equally between the two pulleys. If you want to hold the weight you only have to apply half the weight of the load, i.e. 100/2 = 50 Kgs.

18. A

B will move to the left in this situation.

19. A

B and C will move clockwise as the motor wheel moves clockwise.

20. A

Stack A is the most stable and will therefore support the most weight.

TEST 2
MECHANICAL
COMPREHENSION

YOU HAVE 20 MINUTES TO COMPLETE THIS TEST.

Question 1

If wheel A turns in an anticlockwise direction, which way will wheel B turn?

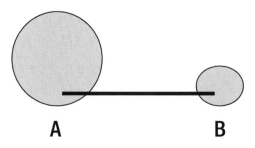

A   B

A. Clockwise

B. Anticlockwise

C. Backwards and forwards

D. It won't move

Answer [   ]

Question 2

Which post is carrying the least heavy load?

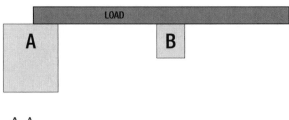

A. A

B. B

Answer [   ]

Question 3

Which pendulum will swing at the fastest speed?

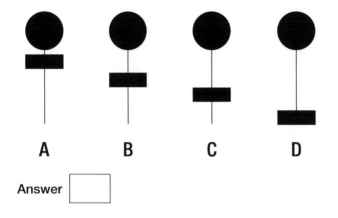

Answer ☐

Question 4

If Cog B turns clockwise, which of the other cogs will also turn clockwise?

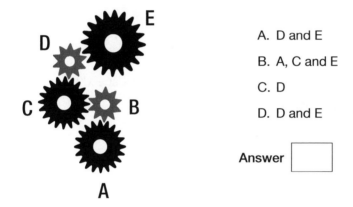

A. D and E

B. A, C and E

C. D

D. D and E

Answer ☐

Question 5

If Cog A moves in a clockwise direction, which way will Cog B turn?

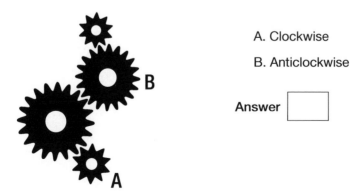

A. Clockwise

B. Anticlockwise

Answer ☐

Question 6

Which shelf will break first when a heavy load is placed on the shelf?

A. Shelf A

B. Shelf B

C. Both the same

Answer

Question 7

At which point will the pendulum be travelling at the fastest speed?

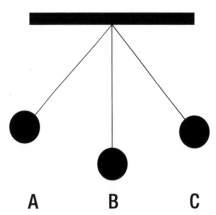

A. Point A

B. Point B

C. Point C

Answer

Question 8

At which point will the beam balance?

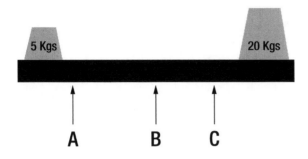

A. Point A

B. Point B

C. Point C

Answer

Question 9

If water is poured into the narrow tube, up to point 'X', what height would it reach in the wide tube?

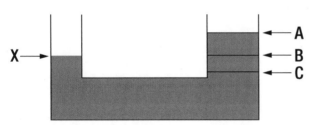

A. Point A

B. Point B

C. Point C

Answer

Question 10

At which point would Ball Y have to be placed to balance Ball X?

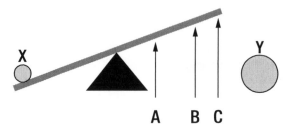

A   B C

A. Point A

B. Point B

C. Point C

Answer [ ]

Question 11

If Cog F rotates clockwise, which way will Cog A turn?

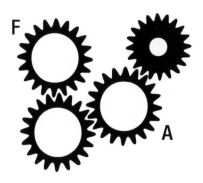

A. Cannot say

B. Clockwise

C. Anticlockwise

Answer [ ]

Question 12

What is the mechanical advantage?

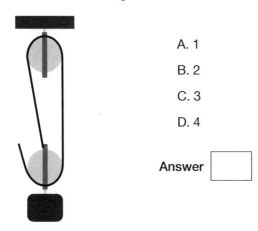

A. 1

B. 2

C. 3

D. 4

Answer [   ]

Question 13

If water is poured in at Point D, which tube will overflow first?

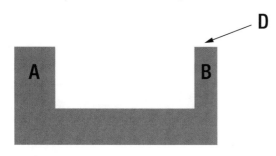

A. Tube A

B. Both the same

C. Tube B

Answer [   ]

Question 14

What is the mechanical advantage?

A. 1

B. 2

C. 3

D. 4

Answer

Question 15

If rope A is pulled in the direction of the arrow, which way will wheel C turn?

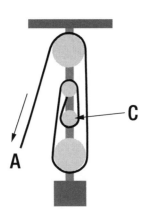

A. Clockwise

B. Anticlockwise

C. It will not turn

Answer

Question 16

Which load is the heaviest?

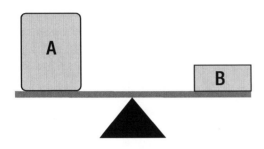

A. Both the Same

B. Load B

C. Load A

Answer

Question 17

If rope A is pulled in the direction of the arrow, which direction will Load Q travel?

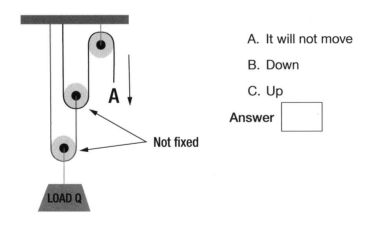

A. It will not move

B. Down

C. Up

Answer

Question 18

If cog A turns anticlockwise at a speed of 20 rpm (revolutions per minute), how will cog B turn?

A. Clockwise 20 rpm

B. Anticlockwise 20 rpm

C. Clockwise 10 rpm

D. Anticlockwise 10 rpm

Answer ☐

Question 19

Which pulley system will be the easiest to lift the bucket of water?

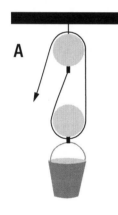
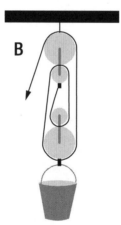

A. Both the Same

B. Pulley A

C. Pulley B

Answer ☐

Question 20

Ball A and B are an identical size and weight. If they are both released at the same time, what will happen?

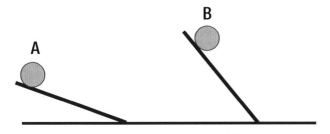

A. Ball A will reached the ground first.

B. Ball B will reach the ground first.

C. They will both reach the ground at the same time.

Answer ☐

Now that you have completed mechanical comprehension exercise 2, check your answers carefully before moving onto the exercise 3.

ANSWERS TO MECHANICAL COMPREHENSION TEST 2

1. B
Because the two wheels are joined they will rotate the same way. If A rotates anticlockwise, wheel B will also.

2. A
Post A is carrying the least heavy load as the majority of force is placed on post B.

3. A
Pendulum A will swing the fastest. The lower down the shaft the positioning of the weight is, the slower the pendulum will swing.

4. C
Cog D is the only other cog which will rotate clockwise.

5. A
Cog B will also rotate clockwise

6. A
Shelf A will break first, simply because the supporting bar is at a shallower angle than B.

7. B
Point B will be the fastest speed. At points A and C the pendulum will be reaching, or have reached, its maximum velocity before falling back down.

8. C
In order to balance the beam the point of balance will move closer to the heavier weight. In this case the 20 Kg weight.

9. B
The water will rise to the same level on the opposite side as point X.

10. A
In order to balance the beam Ball Y will need to be placed closer to the fulcrum point.

11. B
Cog A will rotate clockwise.

12. C
The mechanical advantage of this pulley system is 3. There are three supporting ropes.

 THE **TESTING** SERIES

13. B

Both entrance and exit points of the container are level, therefore, both will overflow at the same time.

14. D

The mechanical advantage of this pulley system is 4. There are four supporting ropes.

15. B

Wheel C will rotate anticlockwise if rope A is pulled in the direction shown.

16. A

Both loads are of equal weight. Do not fall in to the trap of thinking load A is heavier simply because it looks larger. The key to answering this question is to look at the balancing bar. You will see that in this case it is level, meaning that both loads weigh the same.

17. C

Load Q will travel upwards in this situation.

18. A

Cog B will turn clockwise at a speed of 20 rpm.

19. C

Pulley B will be the easiest to lift the load. Pulley A has a mechanical advantage of 2 whereas pulley B has a mechanical advantage of 4.

20. B

Although the distance each ball has to travel is identical, ball B will hit the ground first because the incline is steeper.

TEST 3
MECHANICAL
COMPREHENSION

YOU HAVE 20 MINUTES TO COMPLETE THIS TEST.

Question 1

In the following cog and belt system, which cog will rotate the most number of times in an hour?

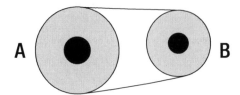

A. Cog A

B. Cog B

C. Both the same

Answer

Question 2

In the following cog and belt system, which cog will rotate the least number of times in thirty minutes?

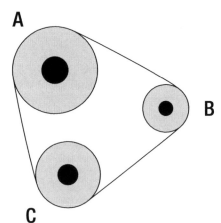

A. Cog A

B. Cog B

C. Both the same

Answer

Question 3

Which rope would require the most effort to pull the mast over?

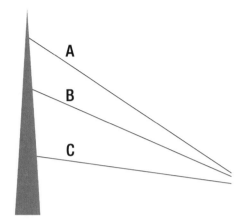

    A. Rope A

    B. Rope B

    C. Rope C

Answer

Question 4

If cog A turns anticlockwise as indicated, which way will cog C turn?

    A. Clockwise

    B. Anticlockwise

    C. Backwards and forwards

Answer

Question 5

If cog A turns anticlockwise, which way will cog D turn?

   A. Clockwise

   B. Anticlockwise

   C. Backwards and forwards

Answer

Question 6

If wheel B moves clockwise at a speed of 20 rpm, how will wheel D move and at what speed?

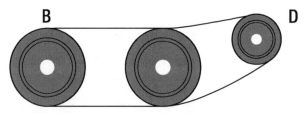

   A. Clockwise faster

   B. Clockwise slower

   C. Anticlockwise faster

   D. Anticlockwise slower

Answer

Question 7

Which is the best tool to use for breaking up concrete?

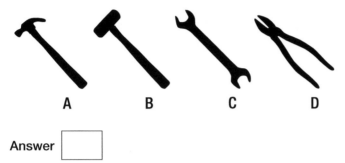

A   B   C   D

Answer

Question 8

In the following circuit, if switch A closes and switch B remains open, what will happen?

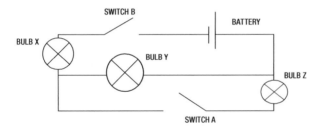

A. Bulbs X, Y, and Z will illuminate.

B. Bulb X will illuminate only.

C. Bulbs Y and Z will illuminate only.

D. No bulbs will illuminate.

Answer

Question 9

In the following circuit, if switch A closes, what will happen?

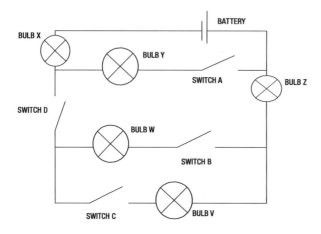

A. Bulbs V, W, X, Y, and Z will illuminate.

B. Bulb X and Y will illuminate only.

C. Bulbs X, Y and Z will illuminate only.

D. No bulbs will illuminate.

Answer [   ]

Question 10

The following four containers are filled with clean water to the same level, which is 2 metres in height. If you measured the pressure at the bottom of each container once filled with water, which container would register the highest reading? If you think the reading would be the same for each container then your answer should be E.

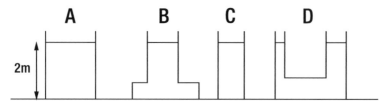

A. A

B. B

C. C

D. D

E. E

Answer

Question 11

You are looking at the following objects side-on. Which is most unstable and likely to topple first? If you think they are all the same then please choose F for your answer.

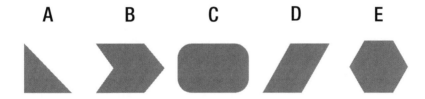

A. A

B. B

C. C

D. D

E. E

F. F

Answer

Question 12

How much weight will need to be placed at point X in order to balance out the beam?

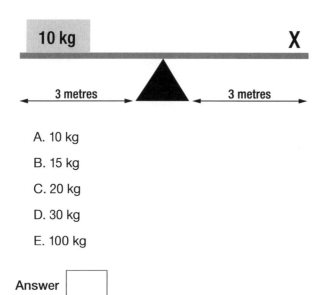

A. 10 kg

B. 15 kg

C. 20 kg

D. 30 kg

E. 100 kg

Answer [   ]

Question 13

If bar A moves to the left, which way will bar B move?

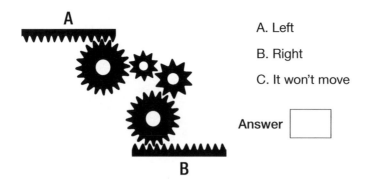

A. Left

B. Right

C. It won't move

Answer [   ]

Question 14

On the following weighing scales, which is the heaviest load?

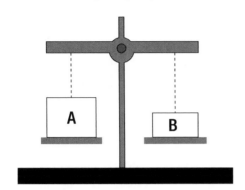

A. Load A

B. Load B

C. Both the same

Answer

Question 15

At which point should pressurised air enter the cylinder in order to force the piston downwards?

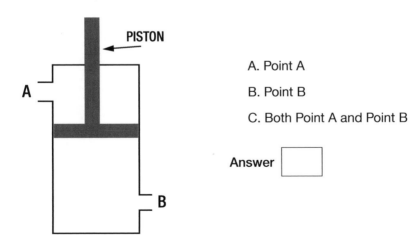

A. Point A

B. Point B

C. Both Point A and Point B

Answer

Question 16

In the following nut and bolt configuration, what will happen to the bolt if you turn the nut clockwise?

A. The nut will move up

B. The nut will move down

Answer ☐

Question 17

At which point will the ball be travelling the fastest?

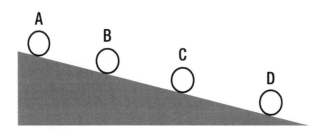

A. Point A

B. Point B

C. Point C

D. Point D

E. The same speed at each point

Answer ☐

Question 18
Will the bulb illuminate?

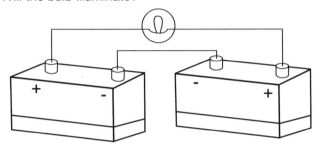

A. Yes

B. No

Answer

Question 19
At which point will the beam most likely balance?

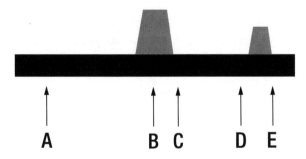

A. Point A

B. Point B

C. Point C

D. Point D

E. Point E

Answer

Question 20

Which is the heaviest load?

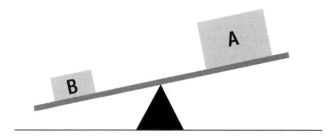

A. Load A

B. Load B

C. Both the same

Answer ☐

Now that you have completed mechanical reasoning test 3, check your answers carefully before moving onto the next section of the guide.

ANSWERS TO MECHANICAL COMPREHENSION TEST 3

1. B

Cog B is smaller and therefore will rotate more times in the given timeframe.

2. A

Because cog A is the largest of the three cogs it will rotate fewer times for any given timeframe.

3. C

The higher up the mast the rope is secured the easier it will be to pull it over. This is because there is more leverage than a rope secured towards the bottom of the mast. Therefore, rope C will require the most effort.

4. B

Cog C will rotate anticlockwise.

5. A

Cog D will rotate clockwise in this configuration.

6. A

Wheel D will also rotate clockwise, but because it is smaller in size it will rotate faster than B.

7. B

Both A and B are suitable for breaking up concrete, however, B (sledge hammer) is designed specifically for this purpose.

8. D

Because the second switch is still open the circuit will remain broken and therefore no bulbs will illuminate.

9. B

Only bulbs X and Y can illuminate in this circuit because the remaining switches remain open.

10. E

The height of the water is level; therefore, the pressure at the base of each container will be equal.

11. D

Out of the objects D is the most unstable and likely to topple first.

12. A

10 Kg must be placed at point X in order to balance the beam.

13. A
Bar B will also move to the left.

14. C
Both loads weigh the same because the scales are evenly balanced.

15. A
Air will need to be forced in at A in order for the piston to move downwards.

16. A
The nut will move upwards.

17. D
At point D the ball will have gained the most velocity and will therefore be travelling the fastest.

18. B
The bulb will not illuminate because the battery is wired incorrectly. For it to illuminate the positive (+) connection should be connected to the negative (-) connection on each battery.

19. C
At point C the beam will most likely balance.

20. B
Load B is the heaviest as the beam is weighing down to the left.

TEST 4
MECHANICAL COMPREHENSION

YOU HAVE 20 MINUTES TO COMPLETE THIS TEST.

Question 1

Which weight requires the most force to lift it?

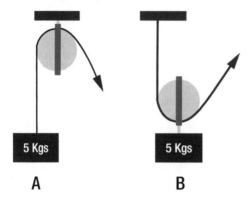

A   B

A. Both the same

B. A

C. B

Answer [   ]

Question 2

How much weight is required to balance point X?

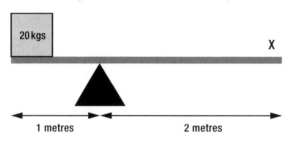

1 metres   2 metres

A. 5Kg

B. 10Kg

C. 15Kg

D. 20Kg

Answer [   ]

Question 3

If cog C turns anti-clockwise at a speed of 10rpm, which way and at what speed will cog B turn?

A. 10rpm / anti-clockwise

B. 10rpm / clockwise

C. 20rpm / anti-clockwise

D. 20rpm / clockwise

Answer

Question 4

Which tool would you use to claw nails from wood?

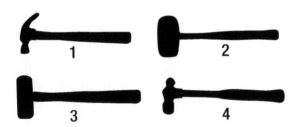

A. 1

B. 2

C. 3

D. 4

Answer

Question 5

If bulb 2 is removed which bulbs will illuminate?

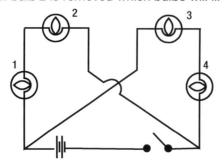

A. 1

B. 3

C. 4

D. None

Answer ⬜

Question 6

When the switch is closed how many bulbs will illuminate when bulb 3 is removed?

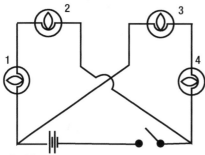

A. None

B. One

C. Two

D. Three

Answer ⬜

Question 7

If cog B turns anti-clockwise which way will cog A turn?

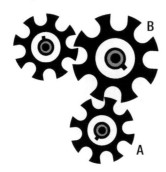

A. Clockwise

B. Anti-clockwise

Answer

Question 8

If wheel A is three times the diameter of wheel B and it rotates at 55rpm, what speed will wheel B rotate at?

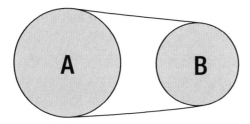

A. 55 rpm

B. 110 rpm

C. 165 rpm

Answer

Question 9

How much force is required to lift the 75 kg weight?

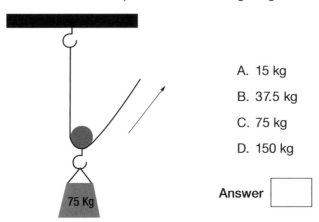

A. 15 kg

B. 37.5 kg

C. 75 kg

D. 150 kg

Answer ☐

Question 10

A screw has 8 threads per inch. How many full turns are required for the nut to travel 3 inches?

    A. 8 turns

    B. 12 turns

    C. 16 turns

    D. 24 turns

Answer ☐

Question 11

Cog A has 12 teeth and Cog B has 18 teeth. If cog B completes two full turns, how many rotations will cog A complete?

A. 3 rotations

B. 2 rotations

C. 1.5 rotations

D. 1 rotation

Answer ☐

Question 12

If cog 4 turns anti-clockwise, which other cogs will also turn anti-clockwise?

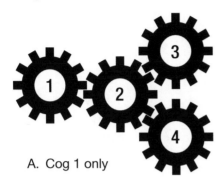

A. Cog 1 only

B. Cogs 1 and 3

C. Cog 3 only

D. Cogs 2 and 3

Answer ☐

Question 13

A thick block of wood rests on an even and level surface. What mechanical principle makes it more difficult to push this block sideways if the surface is made of sandpaper than if it is made of glass?

A. Spring force

B. Gravitational force

C. Air resistance force

D. Frictional force

Answer ☐

Question 14

When water is poured in to a tank, what happens to the pressure on the surface?

A. Decreases

B. Stays the same

C. Increases

Answer

Question 15

The following three HGV's are parked on an incline. Their centre of gravity is identified by a dot. Which of the three HGV's is least likely to fall over?

A. A

B. B

C. C

Answer

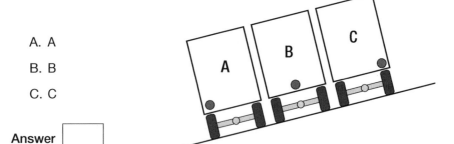

Question 16

Which of the following most resembles a lever?

A. Swing

B. Car

C. Elevator

D. Seesaw

Answer

Question 17

To balance the beam how much weight should be placed on the right hand side?

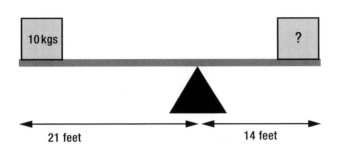

21 feet   14 feet

A. 5 kg

B. 10 kg

C. 15 kg

D. 30 kg

Answer

Question 18

How far from the balance point should the 30 kg weight be placed to balance the beam?

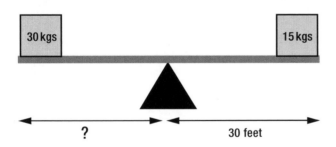

?   30 feet

A. 5 feet

B. 10 feet

C. 15 feet

D. 45 feet

Answer

Question 19

How far would you have to pull the rope up to lift the weight 5 feet?

A. 5 feet

B. 10 feet

C. 15 feet

D. 30 feet

Answer ☐

Question 20

If cog X turns 40 times, how many times will cog Y turn?

A. 40 turns

B. 80 turns

C. 120 turns

D. 160 turns

Answer ☐

Now that you have completed mechanical comprehension exercise 4, check your answers carefully before moving onto the exercise 5.

ANSWERS TO MECHANICAL COMPREHENSION TEST 4

1. B

When answering questions where there is a single pulley system, if the pulley is fixed, as in A, then the force required to lift the weight is the same as the weight, i.e. 5Kg. However, where the pulley system is not fixed and it moves with the weight, as is the case with pulley system B, then the weight required to lift it is half the weight. This means that the weight required to lift B is 2.5kg. The answer to the question is therefore B as pulley system A requires the most weight to lift it.

2. B

Point X is twice the distance from the balance point; therefore, half the weight is required. The answer is B, 10Kg.

3. B

If cog C turns 10 anti-clockwise at a speed of 10rpm then it is relatively straight forward to determine that cog B will rotate the same speed but in a clockwise direction.

4. A

The only tool that you can use from the selection to claw nails from wood is claw hammer A.

5. D

No bulbs would illuminate because the circuit, in its current state, is not working. This is due to the switch being open.

6. C

Only two bulbs would illuminate (bulbs 1 and 2). The broken circuit would prevent bulb 4 from illuminating.

7. A

Cog A will turn clockwise.

8. C

Because wheel A is three times greater in diameter than wheel B, each revolution of A will lead to 3 times the revolution of B. Therefore, if wheel A rotates at 55 rpm, B will rotate at 55 rpm × 3 = 165 rpm.

9. B

This type of pulley system has a mechanical advantage of 2. Therefore, to lift the 75 kg weight will require 75 kgs ÷ 2 = 37.5 kgs.

10. D

There are 8 threads per inch. To move the nut 3 inches will require 8 × 3 = 24 turns.

11. A

Each full turn of cog B will result in 18 teeth ÷ 12 teeth = 1.5 rotations. Two turns of cog B will result in cog A completing 3 rotations.

12. B

Cogs 1 and 3 will also turn anti-clockwise. Cog 2 is the only cog which will rotate clockwise.

13. D

In this particular case frictional force is the force that must be overcome in order to slide the object from one side to another.

14. B

The pressure at the surface remains the same, since it has a finite amount of water above it.

15. A

By drawing a vertical line straight down from the centre of gravity, only the line for HGV A reaches the ground outside of its tyres. This makes the HGV unstable.

16. D

A seesaw is the only option which utilises a form of leverage to function.

17. C

The distance of the weight on the right hand side from the balance point is one third less than the distance on the right hand side; therefore, an additional third weight is required to balance the beam.

18. C.

In order to balance the beam the weight needs to be placed half the distance of the right hand side (15 feet). This is because the weight on the left is twice as heavy as the weight on the right hand side.

19. C

You would need to lift the rope 15 feet in order to lift the weight 5 feet.

20. D

Cog X has a total of 20 teeth, whereas cog Y has a total of 5 teeth. Because cog Y has four times fewer teeth than cog X, it will rotate four times for every single full rotation cog X achieves.

TEST 5
MECHANICAL COMPREHENSION

YOU HAVE 20 MINUTES TO COMPLETE THIS TEST.

Question 1

How many switches need to be closed in order to light up 3 bulbs?

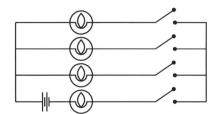

A. 1

B. 2

C. 3

D. 4

Answer [   ]

Question 2

How many switches need to be closed in order to light up 1 bulb?

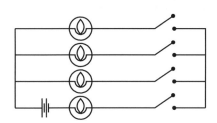

A. 1

B. 2

C. 3

D. 4

Answer [   ]

Question 3

If bulb D is removed how which lights will remain illuminated?

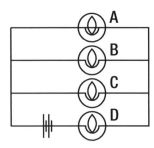

A. Lights A, B and C

B. Lights A and B

C. Lights B and C

D. No lights

Answer [   ]

Question 4

A ball is attached to a piece of string which in turn is secured to a ceiling. The ball and string are then held close to your nose but do not touch it. The ball and string are then released and allowed to swing away from you. When they swing back towards you, will they touch your face if you remain still?

A. Yes

B. No

Answer ☐

Question 5

The glass container at the very top contains water and oil. If you were to now add more water, what would the container look like?

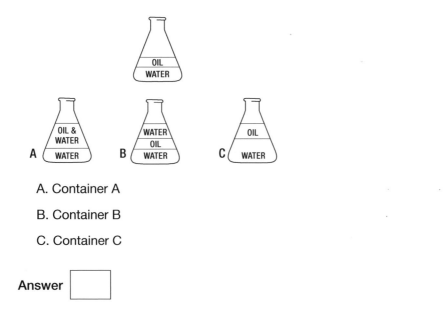

A. Container A

B. Container B

C. Container C

Answer ☐

Question 6

Which spanner will it be harder to tighten the bolt with?

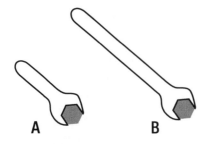

A. Spanner A

B. Spanner B

C. Both the same

Answer [ ]

Question 7

Which stick will be easier to balance?

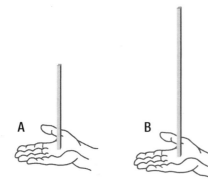

A. Stick A

B. Stick B

C. Both the same

Answer [ ]

Question 8

If wheel 2 is rotating clockwise, which other wheels will also rotate clockwise?

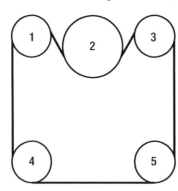

A. Wheels 1, 3, 4 and 5

B. Wheels, 1 and 5

C. Wheels 3 and 4

D. None of them

Answer [ ]

Question 9

If wheel 4 is rotating anticlockwise, which other wheels will also rotate anticlockwise?

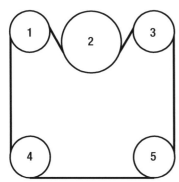

A. Wheels 1, 2, 3 and 5

B. Wheels, 1, 3 and 5

C. Wheels 2 and 5

D. None of them

Answer [ ]

Question 10

If cog B rotates anticlockwise by 10 rotations, how will cog A rotate?

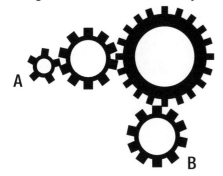

A. Clockwise 5 rotations

B. Anticlockwise 20 rotations

C. Clockwise 20 rotations

D. Anticlockwise 5 rotations

Answer [ ]

Question 11

How far from the fulcrum point would you place the 25 kgs weight in order to balance the bar?

A. 20 feet

B. 15 feet

C. 12 feet

D. 8 feet

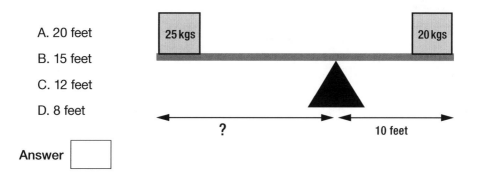

Answer [ ]

Question 12

If bar A moves to the right how will cog B rotate?

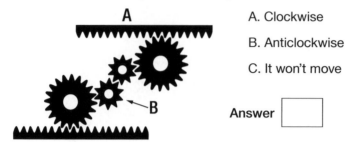

A. Clockwise

B. Anticlockwise

C. It won't move

Answer ☐

Question 13

In order to balance the bar below which way should the fulcrum be moved?

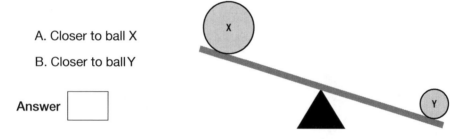

A. Closer to ball X

B. Closer to ball Y

Answer ☐

Question 14

If the large piston has 4 times the surface area of the small piston, how far must the small piston be pushed down in order to raise the large piston 1 cm?

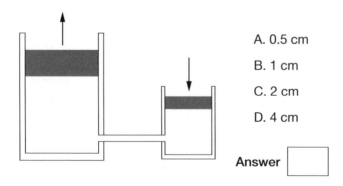

A. 0.5 cm

B. 1 cm

C. 2 cm

D. 4 cm

Answer ☐

Question 15

At what point is the velocity of a bullet fastest?

    A. When it leaves the muzzle

    B. When it reaches the top of its arc

    C. When it hits the target

Answer [ ]

Question 16

If cog B makes 21 rotations, how many will cog A make?

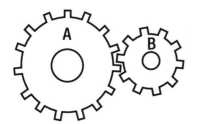

    A. 21

    B. 14

    C. 7

    D. 30

Answer [ ]

Question 17

On which pole is there the most pressure?

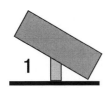 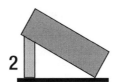

    A. Pole 1

    B. Pole 2

    C. Both the same

Answer [ ]

Question 18

Which term below describes the OPPOSITE of a decrease in speed?

    A. Rotation

    B. Acceleration

    C. Friction

    D. Velocity

Answer

Question 19

A valve is used to perform which of the following tasks?

    A. Control the flow of a liquid

    B. Increase the temperature of a liquid

    C. Facilitate the evaporation of a liquid

    D. Decrease the density of a liquid

Answer

Question 20

A lift is most similar to which of the following mechanical devices?

    A. Spring

    B. Hydraulic jet

    C. Lever

    D. Crane

Answer

 THE **TESTING** SERIES

ANSWERS TO MECHANICAL COMPREHENSION TEST 5

1. C

In order to illuminate 3 bulbs there needs to be at least 3 switches closed.

2. B

In order to illuminate 1 bulb there needs to be at least 2 switches closed.

3. D

If bulb D is removed then the circuit will be broke and no lights will illuminate.

4. B

They will not touch your face because there is insufficient speed or force for the ball to travel further than the point of origin.

5. C

Container C is the correct answer as water is denser than oil.

6. A

Spanner A will be harder to tighten the bolt with, simply because the smaller handle creates less leverage.

7. B

Stick B will be easier to balance because there is more weight at the palm of the hand.

8. D

The only wheel that is rotating clockwise is wheel 2.

9. B

Wheels 1, 3 and 5 will also rotate anti-clockwise, whereas wheel 2 will rotate clockwise.

10. C

Cog A will rotate clockwise 20 rotations. In order to work this out simply count the number of teeth on both cog A and cog B. You will see that cog A has 5 teeth, whereas cog B had 10 teeth. For every one full rotation of cog B, cog A will rotate two full turns.

11. D

The 25 kgs weight would need to be positioned 8 feet from the fulcrum point to balance the bar.

12. A

Cog B will rotate clockwise if bar A moves to the right.

13. B

The fulcrum must be moved closer to ball Y in order to balance the bar. We can assume that ball X is lighter than ball Y; therefore, we need to move the fulcrum closer to Y in order to balance the bar. Do not be fooled by ball X being larger than ball Y and assume that X is heavier. Ball Y is clearly heavier than ball X, despite being smaller in size.

14. D

Because the larger piston is 4 times the surface area the smaller piston will need to be pushed down 4 cm in order to move the large piston 1 cm.

15. A

The bullet will be fastest when it leaves the muzzle. Thereafter, the velocity will decrease.

16. B

Cog A has 15 teeth and cog B has 10 teeth. If cog B makes 21 rotations cog A will make one third fewer.

17. B

There will be more pressure on pole 2 as it is farther away from the resting point.

18. B

Acceleration is the opposite of deceleration.

19. A

A valve is used to control the flow of liquid.

20. D

A crane is similar to a lift in terms of mechanical function.

TEST 6
MECHANICAL COMPREHENSION

YOU HAVE 20 MINUTES TO COMPLETE THIS TEST.

Question 1

Which gate is the strongest?

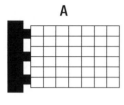 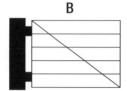

Answer [ ]

Question 2

Which of the following pulley systems has a mechanical advantage of 3?

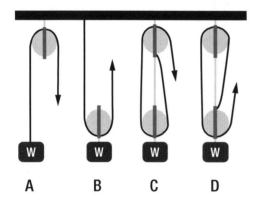

A. A and B

B. C and D

C. B and D

D. D

E. None of them

Answer [ ]

Question 3

Which direction should the wind blow in order for the plane to take off with the shortest runway?

Answer

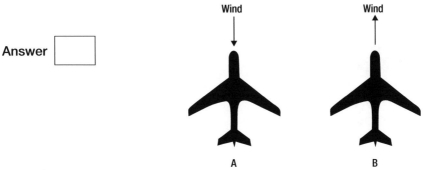

Question 4

Which wheel will rotate the least number of times in one hour?

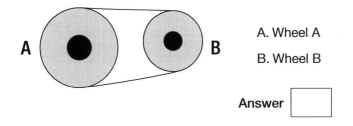

A. Wheel A

B. Wheel B

Answer

Question 5

If cog Y moves anticlockwise which way will cog X move?

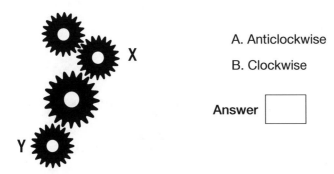

A. Anticlockwise

B. Clockwise

Answer

Question 6

If Cog C rotates clockwise at a speed of 120 rpm, at what speed and direction will Cog A rotate? (rpm = revolutions per minute)

A. 120 rpm clockwise

B. 120 rpm anticlockwise

C. 40 rpm clockwise

D. 40 rpm anticlockwise

Answer ☐

Question 7

A cannonball is fired from a cannon horizontally. At the same time you drop a cannon ball of the same weight from the same height.

Which will hit the ground first?

A. Dropped ball

B. Fired ball

C. Both the same

Answer ☐

Question 8

How much weight in kilograms will need to be added in order to balance the beam?

A. 10 Kg

B. 15 Kg

C. 30 Kg

D. 60 Kg

Answer ☐

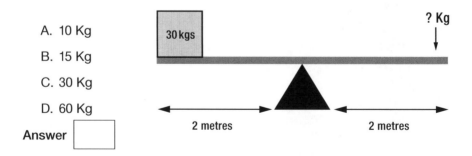

Question 9

How much weight in kilograms will need to be added in order to balance the beam?

A. 10 Kg

B. 20 Kg

C. 40 Kg

D. 80 Kg

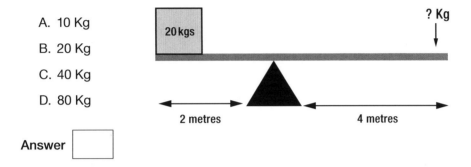

Answer [   ]

Question 10

How much weight in kilograms will need to be added in order to balance the beam?

A. 10 Kg

B. 20 Kg

C. 30 Kg

D. 40 Kg

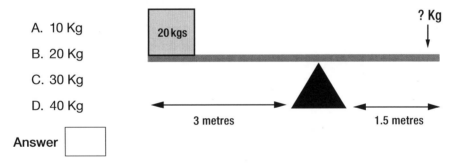

Answer [   ]

Question 11

Which crane is working under the least tension?

A. Crane A

B. Crane B

C. Both the same

Answer [   ]

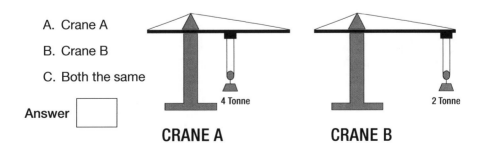

Question 12

Approximately how much force is required in order to lift the load?

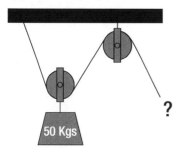

50 Kgs

?

A. 100 Kilograms

B. 50 kilograms

C. 25 Kilograms

D. 5 Kilograms

Answer [   ]

Question 13

If water is poured in at Point X, which tube will overflow first?

X

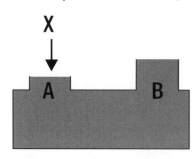

A

B

A. Tube A

B. Both at the same time

C. Tube B

Answer [   ]

Question 14

Which type of beam can take the greatest load?

A

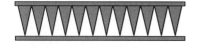

B

A. Beam A

B. Beam B

C. Both the same

Answer [   ]

Question 15

Which cog will make the most number of turns in 30 seconds?

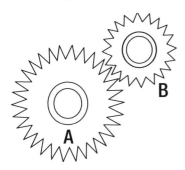

A. Cog A

B. Cog B

C. Both the same

Answer ☐

Question 16

Which load is the heaviest?

A. Load A

B. Load B

C. Both the same

Answer ☐

Question 17

Which tank will not empty?

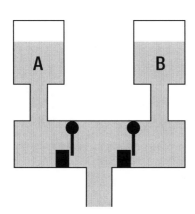

A. Tank A

B. Tank B

C. Both will not empty

Answer ☐

Question 18

If cog Y moves anticlockwise which way will cog X move?

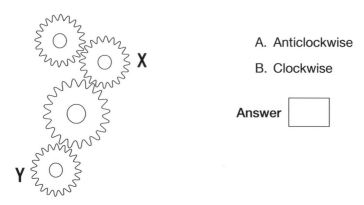

A. Anticlockwise

B. Clockwise

Answer ☐

Question 19

How much weight is required to balance the load?

A. 37.5 Kg

B. 75 Kg

C. 125 Kg

D. 150 Kg

Answer ☐

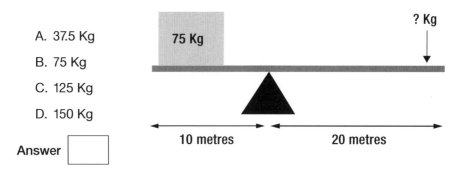

Question 20

At which point(s) should air enter the cylinder in order to force the piston downwards?

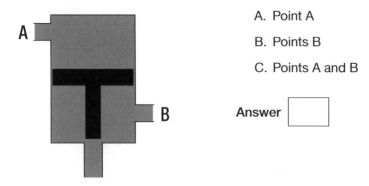

A. Point A

B. Points B

C. Points A and B

Answer ☐

ANSWERS TO MECHANICAL COMPREHENSION TEST 6

1. A

Gate A is the strongest simply because there are more strengthening points in the construction of the gate and there are also three supporting hinges as opposed to two on gate B.

2. D

Only D has a mechanical advantage of 3 as it has three supporting ropes.

3. A

In order to take-off with the shortest runway the aircraft will require a head wind.

4. A

Wheel A is the largest and will therefore rotate the least number of times in any given time-frame.

5. A

Cog X will rotate anticlockwise.

6. A

Cog A will rotate 120 rpm clockwise. When answering questions of this nature it is advisable to count the number of teeth on each. In this particular scenario, each cog has the same number of teeth; therefore, the cogs will rotate at the same speed.

7. C

They will both hit the ground at the same time.

8. C

The distance of the weights from the fulcrum/balance point is identical; therefore, the weight required to balance the beam should be identical.

9. A

The distance of the weights from the fulcrum/balance point is double; therefore, the weight required to balance the beam should be halved.

10. D

The distance of the weights from the fulcrum/balance pint is halved; therefore, the weight required to balance the beam should be doubled.

11. C

They are both under the same tension. Although the weight lifted by crane A is double that of crane B, the weight is closer to the centre of gravity.

12. C

In this type of pulley system the mechanical advantage is 2; therefore, the effort required to lift the load is halved.

13. A

Point A is lower than point B will overflow first.

14. A

Beam A is the strongest because each triangular section covers a greater surface area.

15. B

The cog with the fewest teeth will make the most number of turns in any given time-frame. Because cog B has fewer teeth it will complete more turns that cog A.

16. A

Because the fulcrum/balance point is closer to load A this means that load B must be heavier in order to balance the beam. Therefore, load A is the heavier of the two.

17. B

Tank B will not empty because the valve will not permit water to flow past it.

18. A

19. A

The distance of the weight from the fulcrum/balance point is double; there-fore, the weight required to balance the beam should be halved.

20. A

Air needs to enter at point A in order to force the piston downwards.

Within the final section of this guide I have created 20 sample electrical comprehension tests for you to try. These are not commonplace during mechanical comprehension tests, although they can appear on occasions. Please take your time to work through these questions carefully and try to understand how the answer is reached.

TEST 7
MECHANICAL COMPREHENSION

YOU HAVE 20 MINUTES TO COMPLETE THIS TEST.

Question 1

In the following circuit, if switch A remains open, what will happen?

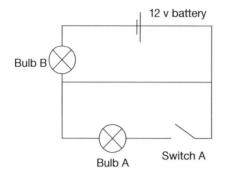

A. Bulbs A and B will illuminate

B. Bulb B will illuminate only

C. No bulbs will illuminate

Answer [ ]

Question 2

Which electrical component is the following a description of?

A safety device which will 'blow' (melt) if the current flowing through it exceeds a specified value.

A. Electron

B. Battery

C. Earth

D. Resistor

E. Fuse

Answer [ ]

Question 3

Identify the following electrical symbol:

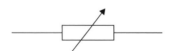

A. Fuse

B. Switch

C. Capacitor

D. Voltmeter

E. Variable resistor

Answer [ ]

Question 4

Identify the following electrical symbol:

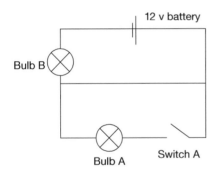

A. Capacitor

B. Ohmmeter

C. Ammeter

D. Bulb

E. Earphone

Answer [ ]

Question 5

In the following circuit, if switch A remains open, what will happen?

A. Bulb A and B will illuminate

B. Bulb A will illuminate only

C. Bulb B will illuminate only

D. No bulbs will illuminate

Answer [ ]

Question 6

Which statement best describes the purpose of the following electrical symbol?

A. Used to measure current

B. Used to measure voltage

C. Used to measure resistance

D. Used to restrict the flow of current

Answer [ ]

Question 7

Identify the following electrical symbol:

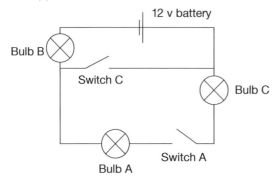

A. Neutron

B. Bulb

C. Inductor

D. Resistor

E. Capacitor

Answer ☐

Question 8

In the following circuit, if switch C remains open and switch A closes, what will happen?

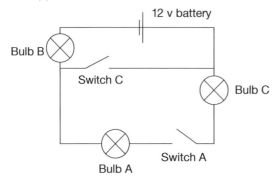

A. No bulbs will illuminate

B. Bulbs A and C will illuminate only

C. Bulbs A, B and C will illuminate

D. Bulb B will illuminate only

Answer ☐

Question 9

In the following circuit, if switches A and B close and switch C remains open, what will happen?

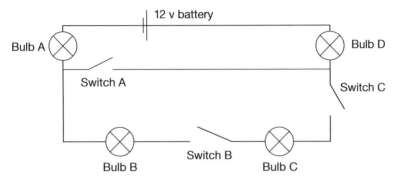

A. No bulbs will illuminate

B. Bulbs A and D will illuminate only

C. Bulbs B and C will illuminate only

D. Bulbs A, B and C will illuminate only

E. Bulbs A, B, C and D will illuminate

Answer

Question 10

Identify the following electrical symbol:

A. AC supply

B. DC supply

C. Motor

D. Transformer

Answer

Question 11

Identify the following electrical symbol:

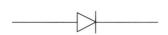

A. Ohm

B. Diode

C. Watt

D. Amplifier

Answer ☐

Question 12

In the following circuit, if switch A remains open and switches B closes, what will happen?

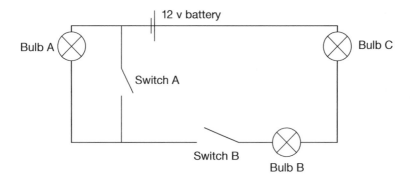

A. No bulbs will illuminate

B. Bulbs A, B and C will illuminate

C. Bulb A will illuminate only

D. Bulbs B and C will illuminate only

Answer ☐

Question 13

In the following circuit, if switch A closes and switch B remains open, what will happen?

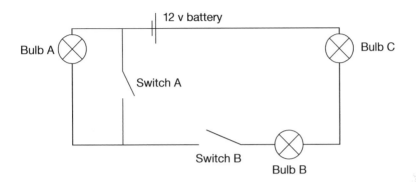

A. No bulbs will illuminate

B. Bulbs A, B and C will illuminate

C. Bulb A will illuminate only

D. Bulbs B and C will illuminate only

Answer [ ]

Question 14

Identify the following electrical symbol:

A. Transducer

B. Bell

C. Heater

D. LED

Answer [ ]

Question 15

What will be the voltage at point X if the battery is 12 volts?

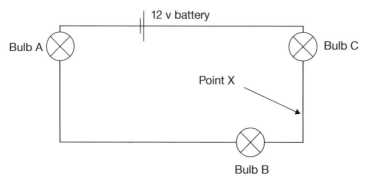

A. 0 Volts

B. 4 Volts

C. 6 Volts

D. 12 Volts

Answer [   ]

Question 16

In the following electrical circuit, if switch B remains open and switches A and C close, what will happen?

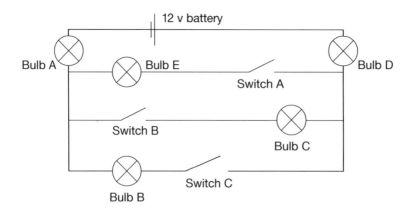

A. Bulbs A, B, C, D and E will illuminate.

B. Bulbs A, B, D and E will illuminate only.

C. Bulbs A, C and D will illuminate only.

D. No bulbs will illuminate.

Answer

Question 17

In the following electrical circuit, if switch B closes, what will happen?

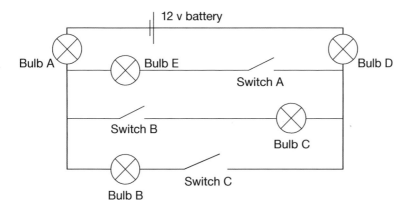

A. Bulbs A, B, D and E will illuminate.

B. Bulbs A, C, D and E will illuminate only.

C. Bulbs A, C and D will illuminate only.

D. No bulbs will illuminate.

Answer

Question 18

In the following electrical circuit, if switches B and C close, what will happen?

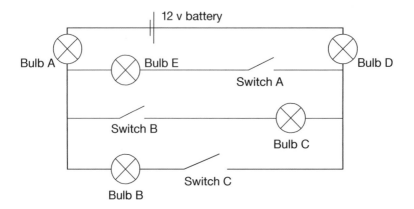

A. Bulbs A, D, and E will illuminate.

B. Bulb E will illuminate only.

C. Bulbs A, B, C, D and E will illuminate only.

D. Bulbs A, B, C and D will illuminate only.

Answer ▢

Question 19

If a fuse blows again after it has been replaced, what is the most likely cause?

A. The resistance in the circuit is too high.

B. The ground point has become disconnected.

C. Open circuit in component.

D. The current through the circuit is too high.

E. All of the above.

Answer ▢

Question 20

A possible cause of an open circuit would be?

    A. A loose component mount.

    B. A pin pushed out of a connector.

    C. A corroded connection.

    D. All of the above.

Answer ☐

ANSWERS TO MECHANICAL COMPREHENSION TEST 7

1. B

In this circuit Bulb B will illuminate only.

2. E

A safety device which will 'blow' (melt) if the current flowing through it exceeds a specified value is called a fuse.

3. E

The symbol is used to identify a variable resistor in an electrical circuit.

4. B

The symbol is used to identify an ohmmeter in an electrical circuit.

5. C

In this circuit Bulb B will illuminate only.

6. A

This symbol is used in electrical circuits to depict an ammeter which is used to measure current.

7. C

The symbol is used to identify an inductor in an electrical circuit.

8. C

Bulbs A, B and C will illuminate as switch A will complete the circuit and make it live once closed.

9. B

Bulbs A and D will illuminate only

10. D

The symbol is used to identify a transformer.

11. B

The symbol is used to identify a diode in an electrical circuit.

12. B

By closing switch B Bulbs A, B and C will illuminate as the electrical circuit will be live.

13. A

No bulbs will illuminate.

14. C

The symbol is used to identify a heater in an electrical circuit.

15. D

The voltage will be the same (12v) throughout the electrical circuit.

16. B

Bulbs A, B, D and E will illuminate only.

17. C

Bulbs A, C and D will illuminate only.

18. D

Bulbs A, B, C and D will illuminate only.

19. D

The current through the circuit is too high.

20. D

A, B and C could all be a possible cause of an open circuit.

A FEW FINAL WORDS

You have now reached the end of the workbook and I sincerely hope you have found the questions useful. Just before you go off and continue your preparation for your assessment, consider the following.

The majority of candidates who pass any career selection process or assessment centre have a number of common attributes. These are as follows:

1. They believe in themselves.

The first factor is self-belief. Regardless of what anyone tells you, you can pass any test or career selection process. Just like anything worth having in life you have to be prepared to work hard in order to be successful. Make sure you have the self-belief to pass your test and fill your mind with positive thoughts.

2. They prepare fully.

The second factor is preparation. Those people who achieve in life prepare fully for every eventuality and that is what you must do when you preparing for your mechanical comprehension test. Work very hard and especially concentrate on your weak areas.

3. They persevere.

Perseverance is a fantastic word. Everybody comes across obstacles or set-backs in their life, but it is what you do about the setbacks that is important. If you fail at something ask yourself 'why' you have failed. This will allow you to improve for next time and if you keep improving and trying, success will eventually follow. Apply this same method of thinking when you set out to achieve anything in life.

4. They are self-motivated.

How much do you want this job? Do you want it, or do you really want it?

When you apply for a job should want it more than anything in the world. Your levels of self-motivation will shine through on your application, at the test centre and also during your interview. For the weeks and months leading up to your assessment or test, be motivated as best you can and always keep your fitness levels up as this will serve to increase your levels of motivation.

Work hard, stay focused and be what you want...

Richard McMunn

 THE **TESTING** SERIES

Notes

Visit www.how2become.com to find more titles and courses that will help you to pass any psychometric test or assessment centre, including:

- Online psychometric tests

- 1 day career training course

- Career guidance books and DVD's

- Psychometric testing books and CDs.

www.how2become.co.uk

 THE **TESTING** SERIES